Privacy in Online Markets: A Welfare Analysis of Demand Rotations

Daniel P. O'Brien

and

Doug Smith[1]

July 2014

Abstract

We compare the private and social incentives for privacy when sellers can commit to transparent privacy policies that are understood by consumers. The purpose is to establish a baseline for how well markets perform when firms' privacy policies are common knowledge. In this setting, if the market is competitive, the outcome is first best or firms provide too much privacy. For monopolized markets, we obtain new results for the welfare effects of demand rotations when preferences over the good and privacy are drawn from the location-scale family, which includes the normal (probit) and logistic (logit) models of demand. We discuss the nature of the distortions and implications for policy toward privacy and the market provision of product attributes generally.

JEL Classifications: D6, D8, L1, L5
Keywords: Privacy, Disclosure, Product Design, Advertising, Demand Rotation, Product Attributes

---

[1]O'Brien: Indiana University and U.S. Federal Trade Commission, Department of Business Economics, Kelley School of Business, Indiana University, 1309 East Tenth Street, Bloomington, IN 47405-1701, obriend@indian.edu. Smith: U.S. Federal Trade Commission, 600 Pennsylvania Ave, NW, Washington, D.C. 20530, dsmith@ftc.gov. The views expressed herein are our own and do not purport to represent the views of the Federal Trade Commission or any Commissioner.

The development of e-commerce raised the economic importance of externalities that arise from the use of customer information. Whereas browsing products in a store or purchasing a product with cash leaves little or no trace of the customer's characteristics, similar activity on the internet can transfer a wealth of information, including: an IP address, email address, home address, and credit card number; a click sequence culminating in the purchase; and a record of a specific purchase by a specific individual.[2] This information is valuable, and its use by the seller or a third party generally affects the customer in some way, e.g., through annoyance factors like spam, or benefits like information about new products. If the exchange of this information is not mediated by price—i.e., if compensation is not conditioned on the use of the information that is transferred—then an externality is present. In this case, the allocation of information and the underlying product or service may be socially sub-optimal.

Both the scope of the problem and the appropriate policy response are the subjects of intense debate. One view is that consumers have a basic right to privacy, and that Congress should pass legislation controlling how customer information is used.[3] Another view is that market forces go a long way toward providing the right amount of privacy in the marketplace, and that the cost of regulation limiting the use of customer information would likely outweigh the benefits.[4]

In the ideal market solution, the legal system would assign property rights over customer information to the buyer or seller, and every transaction that conveys valuable information would also specify compensation to the owner of the property right based on how the information would be used.[5] This solution is efficient if the buyer and seller have complete information and there are no transaction costs (Coase, 1960). However, these assumptions are frequently violated.

In this paper, we develop a simple model of privacy to compare the private and social

---

[2] For an overview of the types of information collected during online activity, see Tucker (2010).

[3] This position is supported by many privacy advocates. See Letter from U.S. NGO's to U.S. Government Leaders Letter from U.S. NGOs to U.S. Government Leaders ("On the Need to Modernize and Update EU and US Privacy Law"), February 4, 2013, available at http://www.centerfordigitaldemocracy.org/digital-privacy.

[4] See, e.g., Lenard and Rubin (2009) for a perspective along these lines. Empirical evidence in Goldfarb and Tucker (2011) shows that privacy regulation in the European Union significantly reduced the effectiveness online display advertising. The policy question is how the reduction in advertising effectiveness affected social surplus.

[5] Varian (1996) suggests this as one possible approach to the privacy problem.

incentives for privacy when an efficient contractual solution is not possible. In our model, the act of purchasing a product or service transfers private information about the customer that is valuable to the seller if it can use the information or sell it to a third party. The product may be a physical good purchased online (for example), or a service like internet browsing activity. (A zero marginal price such as that seen for most browsing activity can arise in equilibrium in our model.) Consumers may have heterogeneous preferences over privacy, with some customers being harmed and some customers benefitting when their information is used. Possible harms include unwanted phone calls, spam, junk mail, higher prices due to future price discrimination, costs associated with identity theft, or simply a dis-utility associated with non-privacy. Possible benefits include receiving more relevant information about future products or services or lower prices from future price discrimination.

Sellers quote prices for their products and make privacy commitments; customers decide whether to purchase based on price and the seller's privacy commitment. Sellers know the distribution of consumer preferences, but not the preferences of specific individuals. Thus, they cannot explicitly condition prices on the customer's taste for privacy. Due to high transaction costs, individual customers cannot make markets for their information by offering to sell it. Therefore, prices do not directly mediate the exchange of customer information between firms and each customer.

We address two main questions. First, in the absence of regulation, do sellers in this environment have the appropriate incentives to offer customers privacy? Second, can privacy regulation increase welfare? We have in mind two types of regulation, one in which the regulator provides the commitment required for firms to offer privacy credibly, and another in which it requires firms to offer specific privacy policies.

Although customer-specific contracts are not feasible in our model, perfect competition yields the first-best allocation under certain conditions. In a competitive equilibrium, the price of the product is conditioned on firms' privacy commitments and indirectly mediates the exchange of information. A requirement for this result is that firms' privacy commitments must be credible. Since firms have a static incentive to renege, a role for the regulator in this case may be to encourage transparency in privacy policies and enforce the privacy commitments that firms make. Another requirement may arise if the value of a customer's information exceeds the marginal cost of making a sale. In this case, the first-best outcome requires a negative price when the product is sold without privacy in order to compensate customers for the value of their information. However, a negative price may not be feasible if customers can exploit it by making multiple purchases under different identities. If a negative price is infeasible, competition can lead to the under-provision of customer information in equilibrium (too much privacy).

Perfect competition provides a useful benchmark, but many online sellers have market power due to product differentiation and/or increasing returns to scale. We address the case of market power by comparing the pricing and privacy incentives of a monopolist to a second-best outcome in which a policy authority can regulate privacy but not price.

Because complete contracts are not feasible in our model, privacy reduces to a product attribute that shifts/rotates aggregate demand at a cost (the opportunity cost of not using the information). Practical results on the welfare effects of monopoly attribute provision are difficult to obtain because the effects generally depend on how demand shifts at all inframarginal quantities (Spence, 1975). We make headway on this issue by focusing on the two-parameter class of demand functions that are linear in the *parameters*, but have arbitrary curvature. This class includes the workhorse models of discrete choice (logit, probit, and linear), as well as representative consumer models in which utility is linear in the parameters. In this setting, privacy often rotates demand as in Johnson and Myatt's (2006) analysis of advertising, marketing and product design. Our analysis of privacy in the monopoly case provides a welfare analysis of the types of demand rotations they studied.

We establish necessary and sufficient conditions for the under- and over-provision of privacy by a monopolist (using a total surplus standard) in the location-scale framework. For markets with interior solutions (incomplete coverage and no binding price constraint), the conditions depend on two simple factors: whether privacy increases or decreases the scale of the gross utility distribution, and whether the ratio of consumer surplus to profit exceeds or is less than the cost pass-through rate. The latter condition is equivalent to whether the *global* incidence of a tax—the incidence of a tax that eliminates the market completely (Fabinger and Weyl, 2013)—exceeds or is less than the *local* incidence of a per-unit tax. Thus, we identify a close relationship between the effects of privacy (or any demand attribute) and tax incidence in the location-scale framework.

We observe that changes in the location parameter effectively shift demand vertically the same way as changing per-unit tax rate, while changes the in scale parameter rotates demand the same way as changing an ad valorem tax rate. Therefore, the effects of privacy in the location-scale framework are analogous to the effects of simultaneously adjusting both types of taxes. If privacy affects only the location parameter—a vertical demand shift—the firm and consumers have the same preferences over privacy. The analogy from the taxation literature is that consumers share the burden of a per-unit tax imposed on a monopolist. If privacy affects the scale parameter, a wedge may exist between private and social incentives that depends on the difference between global and local incidences.

This wedge has a simple interpretation in the location-scale framework, which allows expressing profit and consumer surplus as the product of: (1) scale (i.e., the scale parameter); and (2) a normalized profit or consumer surplus value that depends on scale only through a normalized marginal cost (equivalently a normalized demand intercept). This makes it possible to isolate the effects of scale changes that effectively re-scale marginal cost from those that re-scale the demand function. As with changes that shift demand vertically, consumers share the profit effects of re-scaling marginal cost in proportion to the local per-unit tax incidence. However, consumers share the profit effects of re-scaling the demand function in proportion to the *global* incidence, the ratio of consumer surplus to profit. For example, if the global incidence exceeds the local incidence, then a privacy policy that increases scale but is just unprofitable increases consumer surplus. The firm under-supplies privacy in this case. On the other hand, if the global incidence exceeds the local incidence and privacy reduces scale, then privacy that reduces profit also reduces consumer surplus. The firm does not under-supply privacy in this case. Analogous arguments explain the effects of the wedge in other cases.

A striking result is that the firm, consumers, and the planner have identical preferences over privacy if: demand is linear in price (quadratic utility or uniformly distributed valuations); the market has incomplete coverage in that the fraction of customers that purchase the product is less than 1; and the monopolist's optimal price is not constrained by a lower price bound. Linear demand guarantees that the global and local tax incidences are equal, so that re-scaling demand has the same incidence as re-scaling marginal cost or the demand intercept. The implication of this result is that a divergence between private and social incentives requires at least one of three factors: demand curvature, complete market coverage, and/or a binding price constraint.

The difference between the global and local incidences is nonzero when demand is nonlinear. The difference is positive, for example, if customers' gross utilities have a normal or logistic distribution, as in the probit and logit models of demand. In the normal case, because privacy reduces the variance of the utility component associated with non-privacy externalities, it will reduce the variance (scale) of the gross utility distribution unless the correlation between customer valuations for the product and privacy is sufficiently high. Therefore, our results imply that a necessary condition for the monopolist to under-supply privacy in the case of normally distributed valuations is that the correlation between product and privacy valuations is high enough that privacy increases the variance (scale) of utility distribution.

A binding lower price bound breaks the clean relationships that arise in the unconstrained case. If an unconstrained firm would prefer non-privacy at a negative price but a negative price is infeasible, then the firm may offer some privacy to partially relax the constraint. Given the firm's optimal privacy choice, an additional increase in privacy does not benefit the firm, but it benefits consumers if it shifts demand out by less than required to fully relax the constraint and cause a price increase. We show by example and simulation that the lower price bound increases the likelihood that the monopolist under-supplies privacy, although the frequency and effects of under-supply are relatively small for normally distributed gross utility given flat priors over a reasonable parameter space.

Related Literature.—Most of existing theoretical literature on privacy focuses on the use of customer information to improve matching, screening, or various forms of price discrimination.[6] Varian (1996) and Laudon (1996) appear to be the first to discuss privacy in the context of positive and negative externalities arising from the use or sale of customer information. They also suggest the possibility of a market-oriented solution based on assigning and trading privacy rights. Our paper starts with this perspective and asks how well the

---

[6]Examples include Taylor (2004), Acquisti and Varian (2005), Hermalin and Katz (2006), and Calzolari and Pavan (2006).

market performs when firms hold the privacy property rights, can commit to privacy policies that are understood by consumers, but cannot offer customer-specific prices for their information because preferences are private information.

Privacy mitigates the externalities that non-privacy would impose on customers by rotating demand, as in Johnson and Myatt (2006). It also raises the firm's effective marginal cost by preventing it from capturing the value of each customer's information. These effects are analogous to effects studied in the literatures on quality and advertising, which are also attributes that shift demand and are costly to provide.[7] Although the privacy problem we examine is governed by the same general forces, we obtain new welfare results for demand rotations. Our results have implications for any attribute decisions that shift or rotate demand, such as advertising, product design, and the disclosure of product information that affects utility. Analytically, such disclosure is the flip side of privacy in our framework.

This paper is also related to work on the role of the cost pass-through rate (Bulow and Pfleiderer, 1983) and tax incidence in assessing the welfare effects of firms' decisions (Weyl and Fabinger, 2013). The close relationship between incentives for privacy and tax incidence in our model lends support to the incidence framework set out in Fabinger and Weyl (2013) for understanding the social consequences of private decisions generally. Our monopoly analysis illustrates how the privacy question fits into this framework and provides a detailed analysis when demand is derived from the location-scale family of preference distributions.

Organization of the Paper.—The remainder of this paper is organized as follows. Section I presents the model and characterizes the first best outcome. Section II provides conditions under which Bertrand competition yields the first best solution. Section III studies the monopoly case and establishes conditions under which private and social incentives for privacy diverge for demand functions from the location-scale class. Section IV studies specific cases, illustrating our general results. Section V discusses applications to product attributes other than privacy, and Section VI concludes the paper. Technical proofs not presented in the text are in the Appendix.

---

[7]The seminal works on product quality are Spence (1975) and Sheshinski (1976), which compare a monopolist's incentives for quality provision with those of a social planner. Related contributions in the advertising literature include Dixit and Norman (1978), Kotowitz and Mathewson (1979), Shapiro (1980), and Becker and Murphy (1993) (see Bagwell, 2007 for a survey). Johnson and Myatt (2006) also study advertising but do not conduct a welfare analysis.

I. The Model

We motivate our analysis with a discrete choice framework. However, we interpret our results in the context of other demand structures where appropriate.

There is a continuum of consumers that each receive utility from consuming one unit of a product (or service) and zero utility otherwise. The act of purchasing the product conveys information about the customer that is worth $s > 0$ to the seller if it uses or sells the information after the initial transaction. Consumers are indexed by (v, θ) where v is the value the consumer receives from the product and θ is the benefit the consumer receives if the seller uses or sells its information. We sometimes refer to $-\theta$ as the consumer's privacy valuation. The parameter θ may be positive or negative, reflecting positive or negative externalities from non-privacy (equivalently, negative or positive valuations for privacy). We assume that (v, θ) has a continuous joint distribution $J(v, \theta)$ that is differentiable on the interior of its support, which may or may not be bounded. The joint density function is $j(v, \theta)$. We often refer to the customer that receives the benefit v from the product and θ from the use of its information as "customer (v, θ)." Market size is normalized to 1.

The three key elements of the model are the intrinsic value of the product, the external value of the customer information to the seller, and the external benefit (or cost) to the customer of having its information become public. Most online activity involves these elements. For example, a product purchased online gives the customer a direct benefit, may give the seller access to a range of information about the customer that it can use or sell, and the use of the information may benefit or harm the customer. One can interpret web browsing as the product in this model. Information recorded by the owners of websites and search engines during customer browsing has value for the same reasons as the information collected during the purchase of physical products.

We refer to the situations in which the customer's information will not be used or sold as "complete privacy," and situations when it will be used or sold as "non-privacy." We also model possible intermediate degrees of privacy with a parameter $t \in [0, 1]$, where $t = 0$ indicates non-privacy, $t = 1$ indicates complete privacy, and $t \in (0, 1)$ represents an intermediate degree of privacy. For example, a firm may have a large number of strategies at its disposal to exploit customer information, and $t \in (0,1)$ could represent exploiting the fraction $1-t$ of these possibilities. In cases where the privacy decision is a discrete choice, $t \in \{0,1\}$.

Given privacy level t, the value of using or selling the information is $(1-t)s$, and the benefit consumer θ receives from the privacy component of gross utility is $(1-t)\theta$.[8] If the price of the product is p, consumer (v,θ)'s indirect utility is

$$U(v,\theta,p,t) = \begin{cases} v + (1-t)\theta - p & \text{(Purchase with Privacy Level } t\text{)}, \\ 0 & \text{(No Purchase)}. \end{cases}$$

We examine incentives for privacy when prices are determined by Bertrand competition or monopoly. In each case, the competitors or monopolist quote prices and specify the degree of privacy t (simultaneously under Bertrand competition).[9] A consumer indifferent between purchasing the product or purchasing zero will purchase the product. The marginal cost of production is c.

A. Common Knowledge About Policy Choices

Two important assumptions we make throughout this paper are that firms are committed to the policies they announce, and the policies are transparent to customers in the sense that customers understand them perfectly. Another way to put this is that we assume that a firm's privacy policy is common knowledge.

Our objective in this paper is to examine how well the market performs in environments with privacy concerns when these assumptions are satisfied, either because firms can commit to transparent policies on their own, or because the regulator may facilitate this. The performance of markets for privacy when firms' privacy policies and enforcement practices are not common knowledge is beyond the scope of this paper.

---

[8] The linearity of s in t allows us to interpret t as scaling the benefits and costs of privacy proportionately, but it is not important for our main results. Footnotes 11 and 24 below elaborate on this point.

[9] We are implicitly assuming that it is possible for the seller to keep the information private, and that the customer experiences no benefit or harm if the seller has the information but keeps it private. If the customer receives utility or disutility from having its information in the hands of the seller, then privacy would require anonymizing technology so that the seller would receive no information.

B. The First Best Solution

Before exploring the competitive and monopoly solutions, we consider the first best outcome that a regulator would like to achieve. We assume the planner's objective is to maximize total surplus, the sum of profit and consumer surplus. The firm's profit from a single customer is

$$\pi(v,\theta,p,t) = \begin{cases} p + (1-t)s - c & \text{(Purchase with Privacy Level } t\text{)}, \\ 0 & \text{(No Purchase)}. \end{cases}$$

The planner's objective is to maximize

$$U(v,\theta,p,t) + \pi(v,\theta,p,t) = \begin{cases} v - c + (1-t)(\theta + s) & \text{(Purchase with Privacy Level } t\text{)}, \\ 0 & \text{(No Purchase)}. \end{cases}$$

Purchasing with non-privacy ($t = 0$) is strictly more (less) efficient than purchasing with complete privacy ($t = 1$) if $\theta > (<) - s$, and any level of privacy is optimal if $s + \theta = 0$. Therefore, the first best solution never requires an intermediate level of privacy. Purchasing under complete privacy or non-privacy is efficient if $\max\{v - c, \ v - c + \theta + s\} \geq 0$, and no purchase is efficient otherwise. Intuitively, $v - c$ is the total surplus generated by customer (v, θ)'s consumption of the *product*, and $\theta + s$ is the total surplus generated by its *information* under non-privacy. There is a threshold at $\theta = -s$ such that it is better for individuals with theta above the threshold to purchase without privacy rather than with privacy because the total surplus from the use of their information under non-privacy is positive. It is first best for a customer to purchase the product in its best regime if the sum of the total surpluses from the product and the information in that regime is positive, and it is first-best for the customer to not purchase otherwise. This completely describes the first-best outcome.

II. Implementing the First Best Solution with Competition

In this section, we establish the following result for the effects of competition.

Proposition 1 *Suppose firms can make transparent commitments to keep the information of specific customers private.*

1. Suppose $c - s \geq 0$. Then Bertrand competition yields the first-best outcome.

2. Suppose $c - s < 0$. If a negative price is feasible, then Bertrand competition yields the first-best outcome. If a negative price is not feasible, then competition leads to too much privacy in equilibrium.

The rest of this subsection proves Proposition 1. We first describe the properties of a general first best mechanism. We then show the equilibrium prices that arise under Bertrand competition constitute a first best mechanism.

Let $p(v, \theta, t)$ be transfers from customer (v, θ) to the firm in some mechanism for purchases made at each privacy level t. A customer will choose efficiently between different privacy levels if it internalizes the firm's information benefit, $(1-t)s$. All customers will internalize this benefit if and only if $p(v, \theta, t) + st = p(v, \theta, t') + st'$ for all t, t', and θ. In addition, efficient transfers must compensate the firm for the cost of the product, which implies $p(v, \theta, 1) \geq c$, and they must leave customers who should purchase with non-negative utility, which implies $p(v, \theta, 1) \leq v$. If the customer's efficient choice is non-privacy, these two conditions also ensure that the firm will be profitable, since $p(v, \theta, 1) = p(v, \theta, 0) + s$. Putting these conditions together, a first-best mechanism satisfies:

$$(1) \quad p(v, \theta, 1) \in [c, \max\{c, v\}], \quad p(v, \theta, t) = p(v, \theta, t') + s(t - t') \quad \forall\, t,\, t',\, \theta.$$

It is straightforward to see that the first-best outcome is achieved by Bertrand competition (equivalent to perfect competition in this model) when firms can condition their prices on the degree of privacy.[10] Let $p^B(t)$ be the Bertrand equilibrium prices for each privacy level t. By the usual argument, $p^B(t) = c - (1-t)s$. Formally, any firm charging a price $p > c - (1-t)s$ for the good conditioned on privacy level t will make positive profits if it has any customers, inspiring competitors or entrants to undercut the firm's price by charging a price between p and $c - (1-t)s$. Bertrand competition therefore requires $p^B(t) = c - (1-t)s$. It is easy to see that these prices constitute equilibria.[11] Note that $\{p^B(t)\}$ is a subset of the

---

[10] Note that we are not necessarily requiring each firm to offer to sell the products at more than one privacy level. Some firms may do so, or all firms may specialize. The argument requires that at least two firms have the ability to offer privacy at any level.

[11] In equilibrium, a positive mass of sales can occur only at the end points $t \in \{0, 1\}$ unless the distribution of θ is degenerate at $\theta = s$. This is an artifact of the assumption that the information value is linear

set of first best mechanisms that satisfy the conditions in (1). Thus, Bertrand competition yields the first best outcome. Indeed, it is the first-best outcome in which consumers receive all the surplus.

The reason competition works here is that it leads to different prices for the product under privacy and non-privacy that optimally sort customers into two groups, those that should and those that should not purchase the product with complete privacy. The equilibrium product prices indirectly mediate the exchange of information.

A potentially important caveat to this result is that either $c - s \geq 0$, or there must be a way to make a negative price work in this market. If $c - s < 0$, then with free disposal and the ability to purchase more than once, an individual can repeatedly purchase the good under different identities and effectively sell its information multiple times. If we assume that there is no value in selling an individual's information more than once, the a firm would not offer a negative price under these circumstances. If the lowest price that can be charged is 0 and $c < s$, individuals with $-s < \theta < -c$ will choose to purchase with privacy when it would be strictly more efficient that they purchase without privacy. Too much privacy will be provided in equilibrium. A regulator would need a technology for identifying multiple purchases superior to that of the firms to be able to improve on this outcome.

III. Monopoly

Although perfect competition is a useful benchmark, many sellers on the internet have some degree of market power. We now examine the incentives for privacy under monopoly.

A. Privacy as a Product Attribute

We first derive the monopolist's aggregate demand and profit given price p and privacy level t. Customer (v, θ) will purchase the product iff its gross utility, $u = v + (1 - t)\theta$, exceeds

---

in t. (Neither the result nor the proof is illuminating.) If the value of information were nonlinear in t, then the first best outcome could have interior privacy levels for some customers. Because the effective marginal cost (including the information value) of supplying each privacy level would still be constant, Bertrand competition would supply these privacy levels at the effective marginal cost, supporting the first best outcome.

price. Given the joint distribution $j(v,\theta)$, aggregate demand is therefore

$$D(p,t) = \int_{-\infty}^{\infty} \int_{p-(1-t)\theta}^{\infty} j(v,\theta) dv d\theta.$$

The monopolist's profit is then

$$\pi = [p - (c - (1-t)s)]D(p,t).$$

Inspection of π shows that a marginal increase in privacy shifts demand (by D_t at the margin)[12] and increases the firm's effective marginal cost (by s). The privacy choice appears analogous to a monopolist's advertising choice, as in Dorfman and Steiner (1954), or a quality choice, as in Spence (1975). A difference is that privacy may rotate demand about a price as in Johnson and Myatt (2006), rather than simply shifting demand out.

Our main interest is how the firm's optimal privacy choice compares to the choice a social planner would make. Let $p^*(c,s,t)$ be the monopoly price that maximizes π given (c,s,t). Unlike a social planner, the firm will ignore the effect of its privacy decision on consumer surplus. The effect of a marginal increase in privacy on consumer surplus is

$$
\begin{aligned}
CS_t &= \frac{\partial}{\partial t}\left[\int_{p^*}^{\infty} D(x,t)dx\right] \\
&= \int_{p^*}^{\infty} D_t(x,t)dx - p_t^* D.
\end{aligned}
\tag{2}
$$

Note that here we account for how the firm adjusts price p^* as it changes the level of privacy t. The monopolist's marginal incentive for additional privacy exceeds (is less than) the social planner's incentive as $CS_t < (>) 0$.[13]

In general, CS_t is difficult to sign. This depends on both the inframarginal benefits of privacy, which hinge on how privacy shifts/rotates demand, and the rate at which changes in t are passed into price. The sign of the inequality may also change with t.

B. The Location-Scale Family

To address the monopoly case in a way that is tractable and conducive to empirical analysis, we assume that privacy shifts demand through its effects on the parameters of demand

---

[12] We denote derivatives using subscripts.

[13] This condition is related to the condition given in Spence's Proposition 1. An important difference is that we allow quantity to adjust to monopoly changes in p^* that arise from changes in t, whereas Spence compared private and social incentives for quality at fixed quantities.

functions derived from location-scale family of preference distributions. Specifically, let the cumulative distribution function of u be $F[(u - \alpha(t))/\beta(t)]$ where F is an arbitrary distribution, $\alpha(t)$ is a location parameter that shifts the distribution, and $\beta(t) > 0$ is a scale parameter that affects the distribution's dispersion.[14] This specification includes several common distributions, including the normal, logistic, and uniform, among many others. Under this specification, demand is $D[(p - \alpha(t))/\beta(t)] = 1 - F[(p - \alpha(t)/\beta(t)]$, and inverse demand is $P(q, \alpha(t), \beta(t)) = \alpha(t) + \beta(t)r(q)$ where $r(q) = F^{-1}(1-q)$.[15] If we think of $[u - \alpha(t)]/\beta(t)$ as a measure of the *standardized* utility of a customer that receives utility u, then the customer with standardized utility $r(q)$ is just indifferent between purchasing the product or not, and customers with standardized utilities greater than $r(q)$ purchase the product.

Note that $P(q, \alpha, \beta)$ is also the inverse demand function in a broad class of representative consumer models.[16] Specifically, if the representative consumer has utility function $U(q, \alpha, \beta) = \alpha q + \beta \int_{-\infty}^{q} r(x) dx$, then the customer's optimal quantity choice yields the same inverse demand, $P(q, \alpha, \beta) = \alpha + \beta r(q)$. We frequently refer to this form of demand as being from the location-scale family of preference distributions, but it should be understood that all of our results for demands that are linear in the parameters apply under the representative consumer interpretation as well.

The location-scale family is quite flexible. Changes in the location parameter α cause parallel upward or downward shifts in the inverse demand function, and changes in β rotate inverse demand by changing its slope and possibly its intercept.[17] Demand can have arbitrary curvature through $r(q)$. Under the discrete choice interpretation, the functions $\alpha(\cdot)$, $\beta(\cdot)$ and $r(\cdot)$ are derived from the underlying distributions of v and $(1-t)\theta$. Our assumption is that these distributions are such that the distribution of $u = v + (1-t)\theta$ is in the location-scale family. We provide specific examples in the next section. Under the representative consumer interpretation, these functions can take any form, although we

---

[14]For some distributions (e.g., the normal), α is the mean and β is the standard deviation. In general, the mean is increasing in α, and the standard deviation is increasing in β.

[15]$r(q)$ is the inverse "reliability" or inverse "survival" function that appears frequently in engineering.

[16]We liberally omit the arguments of functions for for brevity when doing so will not cause confusion.

[17]In the uniform distribution, for example, $r(q) = 1 - q$ and $P(q, \alpha, \beta) = \alpha + \beta(1-q)$. Thus, β changes both the intercept and the slope. If the distribution has infinite upper support, the function $r(q)$ does not intersect the vertical axis, so technically there is no intercept.

assume that standard regularity conditions hold. Specifically, we assume that $r(q)$ is twice continuously differentiable and downward sloping, $r_q(q) < 0$, for all $q \in (0,1)$. Our analysis of marginal incentives for privacy assumes that $\alpha(t)$ and $\beta(t)$ are differentiable. We make this assumption where necessary and indicate in specific results when it is not required.

C. Profit and Social Surplus

Working now with the inverse demand, the monopolist's profit is

$$\pi = [\alpha(t) + \beta(t)r(q) - (c - (1-t)s)]q.$$

If we think of $r(q)$ as a standardized inverse demand, a change in the location parameter $\alpha(t)$ is analogous to changing a per-unit tax or subsidy, and a change in scale parameter $\beta(t)$ is analogous to a changing an ad-valorem tax or subsidy. A useful normalization exploited in the literature on taxation is to standardize profit by subtracting $\alpha(t)$ from both price and marginal cost and dividing both by $\beta(t)$.[18] Profit then becomes

$$\pi = \beta(t)\hat{\pi}(q, \hat{c}(t))$$

where $\hat{c}(t) = [c - (1-t)s - \alpha(t)]/\beta(t)$ is the standardized marginal cost,[19] and $\hat{\pi}(q, \hat{c}(t)) = [r(q) - \hat{c}(t)]q$ is the standardized profit. Under this normalization, the full (non-standardized) profit equals the standardized profit scaled by the parameter β. Intuitively, we can think of changes in β as re-scaling a standardized market in which inverse demand is $r(q)$ and marginal cost is $\hat{c}$.

In our model, the monopolist's profit-maximizing price may be negative. This occurs if the inverse demand function intersects the horizontal axis at $q' < 1$ and the customer information information value $(1-t)s$ is sufficiently high.[20] In this case, the effective marginal cost, which decreases with s, may be sufficiently negative that the monopoly price is also

---

[18]For example, Anderson et al. (2001) use this technique to study the relative efficiency of per-unit and ad-valorem taxes. Schmalensee (1984) used a similar normalization to analyze bundling under Gaussian (Normal) demand, a particular case within the location-scale family.

[19]Because the standardized profit is additive in $\hat{c}$ and $r(q)$, an equivalent interpretation is that standardized marginal cost is zero, and changes in $\hat{c}$ shift the intercept of the standardized inverse demand.

[20]For utility distributions with unbounded support, $r(q) \to -\infty$ as $q \to 1$, which implies that $P(q, \alpha, \beta)$ intersects the zero price axis at some $q' < 1$. For distributions with finite support, $P(q, \alpha, \beta)$ may never reach the zero price axis, as in the example in Section IV.B below.

negative. However, negative prices may not be feasible, as discussed earlier. To account for this possibility, we consider cases with and without a constraint requiring the monopoly price to be nonnegative. The monopolist's profit-maximizing quantity solves

$$\max_{q \in [0,1]} \beta(t)\hat{\pi}(q, \hat{c}(t)) \quad s.t. \quad IP[q, \alpha(t), \beta(t)]q \geq 0 \tag{3}$$

where $I \in \{0, 1\}$ is an indicator variable equal to one if a negative price is infeasible and zero otherwise.[21]

Inspection of (3) shows that if the constraint is not imposed or is slack, the effect of t on the optimal quantity comes entirely through $\hat{c}(t)$.[22] We analyze this case first, and consider the case of a binding non-negative price constraint in section IV.E. below.

For the case when the constraint is absent or slack, let $q^*(\hat{c}(t))$ be the monopoly quantity, and let $\hat{\Pi}(\hat{c}(t)) = \hat{\pi}(q^*(\hat{c}(t)))$ be the maximized value of $\hat{\pi}$. The full (non-standardized) profit at the monopoly solution is then

$$\Pi(t) = \beta(t)\hat{\Pi}(\hat{c}(t)). \tag{4}$$

Consumer surplus for any quantity q is

$$\int_0^q (\alpha + \beta r(x))dx - (\alpha + \beta r(q))q = \beta \left(\int_0^q r(x)dx - r(q)q \right).$$

Thus, consumer and total surplus at the profit-maximizing quantity are given by

$$CS(t) = \beta(t)\hat{CS}(\hat{c}(t)), \tag{5}$$

$$TS(t) = \beta(t)\hat{TS}(\hat{c}(t)) \tag{6}$$

where

$$\hat{CS}(\hat{c}) = \int_0^{q^*(\hat{c})} r(q)dq - r(q^*(\hat{c}))q^*(\hat{c})$$

is the standardized consumer surplus, and $\hat{TS}(\hat{c}) = \hat{CS}(\hat{c}) + \hat{\Pi}(\hat{c})$ is the standardized total surplus. We see that in the location-scale framework, all the surplus values are scaled versions of standardized values. We sometimes refer to the scaling factor β simply as "scale" to reflect its role scaling the size of each surplus value.

---

[21] The constraint $IPq \geq 0$ is the same as the constraint $IP \geq 0$ for $q > 0$. Writing the constraint this way will be useful later.

[22] This follows because $\beta(t)$ is independent of q.

We use the following definition to describe local *under-supply* or *over-supply* of privacy by the monopolist.

Definition 1 *The monopolist locally under-supplies or over-supplies privacy if the following conditions are satisfied:*

$$\text{Under-supply} \iff \Pi_t \leq 0 < TS_t,$$
$$\text{Over-supply} \iff TS_t < 0 \leq \Pi_t.$$

In some cases the over-/under-supply question pertains to discrete changes in privacy rather than marginal changes. Define $\Delta CS = CS(1) - CS(0)$ as the change in consumer surplus in going from non-privacy to complete privacy; define ΔTS and $\Delta \Pi$ analogously. The monopolist under-supplies or over-supplies complete privacy if these discrete analogs of the conditions in Definition 1 hold.

D. Welfare Analysis in the Unconstrained Case

Equations (4), (5), and (6) show that when the non-negative price constraint is absent or slack, the monopoly profit, consumer surplus, and total surplus are equal to their respective standardized values scaled by the same factor, $\beta(t)$. These equations also show that the effect of privacy on each standardized surplus value comes entirely through its effect on the standardized marginal cost, $\hat{c}$. At an interior solution $q^* \in (0,1)$, the derivatives of the standardized surplus values with respect to $\hat{c}$ are

$$(7) \qquad \hat{\Pi}_{\hat{c}} = -q^*, \quad \hat{CS}_{\hat{c}} = -\tau q^*, \quad \hat{TS}_{\hat{c}} = -(1+\tau)q^*$$

where $\tau = r_q q^*_{\hat{c}} = -1/(r_{qq} q^* + 2r_q)$ is the cost pass-through rate—the rate at which a small increase in marginal cost leads to an increase in price. The pass-through rate is positive by standard arguments. Because all standardized surplus values are decreasing in $\hat{c}$ at an interior solution, we have the following proposition.

Proposition 2 *Suppose a marginal change in privacy does not affect scale (i.e., β does not vary with t). Then if the monopolist is not constrained by a zero lower price bound and the market is not covered ($q^* < 1$), the privacy preferences of the monopolist, consumers, and* *the planner are perfectly aligned. That is, for all functions $\alpha(t)$ and $\beta(t)$, the firm prefers privacy choice t' over choice t if and only if consumers and the planner also prefer t' over t.*

Proposition 2 has a direct analog in the taxation literature. When β does not depend on t, the effect of privacy comes entirely through $\hat{c}(t)$, and a change in a constant marginal cost is analogous to changing a per-unit tax. Under monopoly, a standard result is that a monopolist and consumers share the burden of a per-unit tax.[23] This is essentially what Proposition 2 says.[24]

An additional analogy with taxation emerges from the conditions in (7). When $\beta_t = 0$, $CS_t/\Pi_t = (CS_{\hat{c}}\hat{c}_t)/(\Pi_{\hat{c}}\hat{c}_t) = \tau$, using (7). This shows that τ measures the *local incidence* of an increase in privacy when $\beta_t = 0$. In the taxation literature, the cost pass-through rate is identified with the local incidence of a per-unit tax.[25] This implies the following corollary.

Corollary 1 *Suppose a marginal change in privacy does not affect scale ($\beta_t = 0$). Then, if the monopolist is not constrained by a zero lower price bound and the market is not covered ($q^* < 1$), the local incidence of privacy, CS_t/Π_t, equals the local incidence of a per-unit tax.*

To obtain a sharper prediction, differentiate Π and CS with respect to t and substitute from (7) to obtain

$$\Pi_t = \beta_t \hat{\Pi} + \beta \hat{\Pi}_{\hat{c}} \hat{c}_t$$
$$(8) \qquad = \beta_t \hat{\Pi} - \beta q^* \hat{c}_t$$
$$CS_t = \beta_t \hat{CS} + \beta \hat{CS}_t$$
$$(9) \qquad = \beta_t \hat{CS} - \beta \tau q^* \hat{c}_t.$$

---

[23] This is Principle of Incidence (Monopoly) 2, Fabinger and Weyl (2013).

[24] Proposition 2 and the other results in this section do not depend on the linear relationship between the information value and t that we have assumed to simplify our presentation. What matters is that changes in the information value affect profits only through the standardized marginal cost, $\hat{c}(t)$. This will be true under any relationship between the information value and t such that the expected information value is the same for each customer.

[25] Principle of Incidence (Monopoly) 3, Fabinger and Weyl (2013).

Solving (8) for $\hat{c}_t$, substituting into (9), and rearranging yields

$$CS_t = \beta_t \hat{\Pi} \left[\frac{\hat{CS}}{\hat{\Pi}} - \tau \right] + \tau \Pi_t \tag{10}$$

$$= \frac{\beta_t}{\beta} \Pi \left[\tau^G - \tau \right] + \tau \Pi_t \tag{11}$$

where $\tau^G = \hat{CS}/\hat{\Pi} = CS/\Pi$ is called the *global incidence* by Fabinger and Weyl (2013). The global incidence is the incidence of a tax (or any policy) that completely eliminates the market. Adding Π_t to CS_t yields the derivative of total surplus at the monopoly solution,

$$TS_t = \frac{\beta_t}{\beta} \Pi \left[\tau^G - \tau \right] + (1+\tau)\Pi_t. \tag{12}$$

Conditions (10) through (12) characterize the relationship between private and social incentives for privacy under monopoly when demand is from the location-scale family.

Under linear demand (uniformly distributed u or quadratic utility) and constant marginal cost, it is well known that $\hat{CS}/\hat{\Pi} = \tau^G = \tau = 1/2$ at an interior solution.[26] In this case, the terms in square brackets in (10) through (12) are zero. This means that TS_t and CS_t are both proportional to Π_t, so that under linear demand, private and social preferences for privacy are perfectly aligned. Although these equations assume that the parameters are differentiable in t, this assumption is not required for preference alignment under linear demand.[27] The following proposition states the result.

Proposition 3 *Suppose the $r(q)$ is linear. Then, if the monopolist is not constrained by a zero lower price bound and the market is not covered ($q^* < 1$), the privacy preferences of the monopolist, consumers, and the regulator are perfectly aligned. That is, for all functions $\alpha(t)$ and $\beta(t)$, the firm prefers privacy choice t' over choice t if and only if consumers and the planner also prefer choice t' over choice t.*

Although this result is simple, it does not appear to have received significant attention in the literature on product attributes. The implication here is that any divergence between private and social incentives for privacy requires at least one of three conditions to

---

[26] See Bulow and Pfleiderer (1983).

[27] Under linear demand and constant marginal cost, consumer surplus, and total surplus are proportional to the square of the monopoly quantity at an interior solution. Specifically, $\Pi = q^*(\hat{c}(t))^2$, $CS = q^*(\hat{c}(t))^2/2$, and $TS = 3q^*(\hat{c}(t))^2/2$. Therefore, the firm, consumers, and the planner have the same preferences over t for arbitrary functions $\alpha(t)$ and $\beta(t)$.

hold: nonlinear demand, the monopoly price is constrained, and/or the market is completely covered.

The following proposition characterizes the scope for misalignments between private and social incentives that arise from nonlinearities of $r(q)$ at interior monopoly solutions. The proposition follows from (12) and the definitions of the functions in that expression.

Proposition 4 *Suppose the monopolist is not constrained by a zero lower price bound and the market is not covered ($q^* < 1$).*

1. *Necessary conditions.*

   (a) *If $\beta_t < 0$ and $\tau^G \geq \tau$, the monopolist does not under-supply privacy.*

   (b) *If $\beta_t < 0$ and $\tau^G \leq \tau$, the monopolist does not over-supply privacy.*

   (c) *If $\beta_t > 0$ and $\tau^G \geq \tau$, the monopolist does not over-supply privacy.*

   (d) *If $\beta_t > 0$ and $\tau^G \leq \tau$, the monopolist does not under-supply privacy.*

2. *Sufficient conditions. If $|\tau^G - \tau| > 0$ and $|\beta_t| > 0$, then there exist parameter values such that the firm either under-supplies or over-supplies privacy.*

At interior solutions, a misalignment between private and social incentives for privacy requires two conditions: the global and local tax incidences must diverge, and privacy must change the scale of the distribution. When both conditions hold, a wedge $(\beta_t/\beta)\Pi[\tau^G - \tau]$ exists between private and social incentives, and the distortion depends on the signs of the scale change β_t and the difference between the global and local tax incidences, $\tau^G - \tau$. This is explained as follows. A change in scale, β_t, affects standardized profit $(r(q) - \hat{c})q$ by re-scaling the standardized marginal cost $\hat{c}$ (or the standardized demand intercept) and the standardized inverse demand $r(q)$. Consumers share the effect on the standardized marginal cost in proportion to the local incidence, which is $-\tau$ for a cost increase. Consumers share the effect on $r(q)$ in proportion to the global incidence, τ^G. The global incidence incorporates the fact that re-scaling the entire inverse demand curve shifts it up or down by different amounts at different quantities if the curve is non-linear. This is why non-linearities give rise to distortions in location scale framework. Changes in scale affect inframarginal consumers differently than they affect the marginal consumer when demand is non-linear.

For the two most commonly-employed distributions in discrete choice, the normal and logistic, $\tau^G - \tau > 0$ for all values of $\hat{c}$.[28] For these distributions, the applicable conditions in Proposition 4 are 1a and 1c. The firm will not under-supply privacy (but may over-supply it) if privacy reduces scale, and the firm will not over-supply privacy (but may under-supply it) if privacy increases scale. In the next section, we present an illustration using the normal distribution.

A seminal paper by Spence (1975) showed that a monopolist's marginal incentive to increase quality *holding quantity fixed* is greater than (less than) the social incentive if the average benefit to inframarginal consumers from the quality increase is greater than (less than) the benefit to the marginal consumer. The difference between the global and local incidence that arises in our analysis is analogous to the difference in benefits to inframarginal and marginal consumers in Spence. However, the incidence analysis also accounts for how the equilibrium quantity changes, whereas Spence's analysis did not.

E. Welfare Analysis with a Constraining Zero Lower Price Bound

The marginal price of some services offered over the internet (e.g., browsing) is zero. It is possible that firms would like to offer negative prices to subsidize such services but do not do so because customers would exploit this in ways that would be unprofitable. We now examine the consequences of a binding non-negative price constraint on the welfare analysis of privacy effects under monopoly.

The Lagrangian for the monopolist's maximization problem in (3) can be written

$$\mathcal{L} = [\alpha(t) + \beta(t))r(q) - (c - (1-t))s]q + \lambda[\alpha(t) + \beta(t)r(q)]q$$

where $\lambda(t) \geq 0$ is the shadow cost of tightening the price constraint at the monopolist's constrained optimal quantity. Note that $1 + \lambda(t)$ is a multiplicative factor with respect to both $\alpha(t)$ and $\beta(t)$ in $\mathcal{L}$. This suggests modifying the normalization procedure used in the

---

[28] Fabinger and Weyl's (2012) classification of distributions used in discrete choice models by their pass-through properties shows that the pass-through rates for the normal and logistic distributions are increasing in marginal cost. This implies that the global incidence exceeds the local incidence.

unconstrained case by subtracting $\alpha(t)(1 + \lambda(t))$ from price and cost and dividing both by $\beta(t)(1 + \lambda(t)) \equiv \eta(t)$. This normalization yields

$$\mathcal{L} = \eta(t)\hat{\pi}(q, \bar{c}(t))$$

where $\bar{c}(t) = [c - (1 - t)s - \alpha(t)(1 + \lambda(t))]/\eta(t)$ and $\hat{\pi}(q,\bar{c}) = [r(q) - \bar{c}(t)]q$. Given this normalization, the difference between the constrained and unconstrained cases is that the monopoly quantity depends on a different standardized marginal cost, $\bar{c}$, and monopoly profit (equal to $\mathcal{L}$) has a different effective scale factor, $\eta(t) = \beta(t)(1 + \lambda(t))$. Both terms account for the shadow cost of tightening the constraint, $\lambda(t)$. Let $\bar{q}(\bar{c}(t))$ be the monopolist's profit maximizing quantity. Consumer and total surplus have the same scale factor $\beta(t)$ as before, but the effects of privacy flow through $\bar{q}(\bar{c}(t))$ rather than $q^*(\hat{c}(t))$. Thus, in the constrained case, the surplus values at the monopoly solution are

(13) $$\overline{\Pi} = \eta(t)\hat{\Pi}(\bar{c}(t))$$

(14) $$\overline{CS} = \beta(t)\hat{CS}(\bar{c}(t))$$

(15) $$\overline{TS} = \beta(t)\hat{TS}(\bar{c}(t))$$

Differentiating $\overline{\Pi}$ and $\overline{CS}$ with respect to t and eliminating $\bar{c}_t$ yields the following analog of expression (12):

(16) $$\overline{CS}_t = \frac{\eta_t}{\eta}\overline{\Pi}\left[\tau^G E^\beta_\eta - \frac{\beta}{\eta}\tau\right] + \frac{\beta}{\eta}\tau\overline{\Pi}_t.$$

In (16), $E^\beta_\eta = (\beta_t/\beta)(\eta_t/\eta) = (\partial\beta/\partial\eta)(\eta/\beta)$ is the elasticity of actual scale, β, with respect to the firm's effective scale, η. It is easy to see that (16) reduces to (12) when the constraint does not bind.[29]

The analogs of Propositions 2 and 4 without the lower price bound qualification hold with η_t replacing β_t and the adjusted incidence difference $\tau^G E^\beta_\eta - (\beta/\eta)\tau$ replacing $\tau^G - \tau$. However, it is more illuminating to understand how the constraint alters incentives relative to the unconstrained case.

We first present an intuitive argument illustrating how the constraint expands the scope for distortions, and then we relate the intuition to condition (16). Suppose the non-negative

---

[29]In this case, $\lambda = 0$, and thus $\eta = \beta$, $E^\beta_\eta = 1$, $\hat{c}(t) = \bar{c}(t)$, and $q^*(\hat{c}) = \bar{q}(\bar{c})$, which implies $\overline{CS}_t = CS_t$ and $\overline{\Pi}_t = \Pi_t$.

price constraint binds strictly, and let $\bar{t} = \arg\max_t \overline{\Pi}(t)$. Because the constraint binds, $\bar{t} < 1$. (If $\bar{t} = 1$, marginal cost would be positive and the constraint would not bind.) Now introduce a small increase in privacy Δt that shifts inverse demand up by an amount $\alpha_t \Delta t$ (assuming $\alpha_t > 0$) that is too small to fully relax the constraint. If the monopolist were required to make this change, it would continue charging a price of zero, and consumer surplus would increase by approximately $\alpha_t \Delta t \bar{q} > 0$. The monopolist under-supplies privacy if $\alpha_t \Delta t \bar{q} > -\overline{\Pi}_t \Delta t$. This inequality certainly holds if the monopolist's choice of t is an interior solution, as $\overline{\Pi}_t = 0$ in that case. If $\bar{t}$ is a corner solution at $t = 0$, then the under-supply question depends on the relative surplus changes.

The distortion identified in this example does not require nonlinear demand, which means that the analog of Proposition 3 does *not* hold when the global and local incidences are equal. This is clear from equation (16), which shows that equality between the global and local incidences zeros out the bracketed term only if $E_\eta^\beta = \beta/\eta$, which is not generally true under a binding price constraint. The example emerges from equation (16) after incorporating the assumptions into the equation. Suppose the shadow cost of the constraint is decreasing in t, i.e., $\lambda_t < 0$. This is certainly true for some t, as raising t eventually relaxes the constraint. If $\beta_t = 0$ and $\lambda_t < 0$, then $\eta_t = \beta_t(1+\lambda) + \beta\lambda_t < 0$ and $E_\eta^\beta = 0$. The first term in (16) is then positive, and the second term is weakly negative by the assumption that $\bar{t}$ maximizes profits. If the second term in (16) is small enough in absolute value, then it follows from the equation that the monopolist under-supplies privacy at the margin.

The following proposition provides a more general result that encompasses this example.

Proposition 5 *Suppose the monopolist is constrained by a binding non-negative price constraint, the market is not completely covered, and $\beta_t = 0$.*

1. *If $\lambda_t \leq 0$, the monopolist does not over-supply privacy.*

2. *If $\lambda_t \geq 0$, the monopolist does not under-supply privacy.*

If demand is linear, then there exist values of (α_t, s) such that the monopolist under-supplies privacy.

Obviously, distortions can also arise in the case of a binding lower price constraint when $\beta_t \neq 0$. Proposition 5 indicates that the conditions that guarantee the alignment of private and social preferences in Propositions 2 and 3 do not guarantee this alignment when the monopolist is bound by a non-negative price constraint.

F. Fixed Costs of Privacy

We have assumed that the cost of privacy is limited to the forgone value of customer information that is not used or sold. Under this assumption, privacy affects marginal cost, but not fixed cost. We now show how the welfare results change if the degree of privacy also affects fixed costs. We discuss the case when the non-negative price constraint is slack and the monopolist's profit-maximizing quantity is an interior solution. The analysis for the case when the constraint binds is similar but with the modified normalization that accounts for the constraint.

Let $K(t)$ be the fixed cost of providing privacy level t. The profit-maximizing quantity is still $q^*(\hat{c}(t))$, as it does not depend on $K(t)$, and consumer surplus is still $CS(t) = \beta(t)\hat{CS}(\hat{c}(t))$. However, the maximized profit is now $\Pi(t) = \beta(t)\hat{\Pi}(\hat{c}(t)) - K(t)$.[30] Following the same procedure as above to relate the change in total surplus to the change in profit, the analog of (12) is now

$$(17) \qquad TS_t = \frac{\beta_t}{\beta}[\Pi + K]\left[\tau^{GV} - \tau\right] + (1+\tau)\Pi_t + \tau K_t.$$

where $\tau^{GV} = \hat{CS}/\hat{\Pi} = CS/(\Pi + K)$ is the global incidence based on variable profit, which excludes (adds back) the fixed cost K.

Compared to the case with no fixed cost, even if the wedge $(\beta_t/\beta)[\Pi + K][\tau^{GV} - \tau]$ is zero, another distortion arises from the additional term τK_t. If $\beta_t = 0$ or demand is linear (conditions that ensure first term on the right side of (17) is zero), the monopolist will undersupply privacy if $\Pi_t \leq 0$ and $K_t > -\Pi_t(1+\tau)/\tau$, and it will over-supply privacy if the opposite inequalities are true. A sufficient condition for under-supply when the scale/incidence term is zero is that the profit-maximizing privacy choice is an interior solution ($\Pi_t = 0$) and $K_t > 0$.

The logic behind this result is that the monopolist bears the full burden of privacy-induced changes in fixed cost, but it bears only a $1/(1+\tau)$ share of the surplus change from

---
[30]The normalization procedure is the same as before, but it is not applied to $K(t)$.

privacy-induced changes in α and β. This means that a change in privacy that affects fixed costs but has no effect on profit will generally raise or lower total surplus.

We have emphasized the effects of privacy on the information value (marginal cost) rather than fixed costs for two main reasons. First, we have no firm basis for mapping privacy changes that affect the location and scale of gross utility into changes in fixed costs. Second, there is a clear basis for assigning positive value to the information content associated with each individual's participation in an activity. We return to the fixed cost case in our discussion of the the implications of our results for advertising in Section V below.

IV. Specific Cases under Monopoly

We now examine specific cases that illustrate our monopoly results and provide some perspective on the direction and magnitude of the distortions. The first two cases assume that customer heterogeneity arises from either disperse preferences for the product (case A) or disperse preferences for privacy (case B), but not both. These cases are of interest to illustrate simple environments in which changes in privacy affect surplus values by changing the parameters of demand functions derived from the location-scale family. The third case (C) provides an example with linear demand and correlated values for the product and privacy. The fourth case (D) assumes that valuations for the product and privacy have a multivariate normal distribution. This is a rich case that illustrates the full range of our results.

A. Common Non-Privacy Externality

Suppose that $\bar{\theta}$ is a common externality experienced by all consumers, and that v has an arbitrary distribution with cumulative distribution function $F(v)$. This is a simple Hotelling-style model in which customer heterogeneity arises from disperse preferences for the product. The distribution of $u = v + (1-t)\bar{\theta}$ is $F(u - (1-t)\bar{\theta})$. It is readily apparent that $F(\cdot)$ is a location-scale family with $\alpha(t) = (1-t)\bar{\theta}$, $\beta(t) = 1$, and inverse demand $P(q,t) = (1-t)\bar{\theta} + r(q)$ where $r(q) = F^{-1}(1-q)$.

Because privacy shifts only the location parameter (the intercept), Proposition 2 implies that private and social preferences are aligned at an interior solution.[31] That is, consumer and total surplus both rise (fall) with privacy if and only if profits also rise (fall).

Binding Non-Negative Price Constraint.—The common externality case is useful for illustrating the effects of a non-negative pricing constraint in an analytically tractable model. To isolate distortions caused by the constraint, we make assumptions that yield linear demand. Specifically, suppose v is uniformly distributed on the interval $[0,1]$. Then $u = v + (1-t)\bar{\theta}$ is uniformly distributed on $[(1-t)\bar{\theta}, 1+(1-t)\bar{\theta}]$, and inverse demand is $P(q,t) = 1 + (1-t)\bar{\theta} - q$. Assume without loss of generality that $c = 0$.

Straightforward calculations show that conditional on t, the unconstrained monopoly quantity and profit are $q^*(t) = [1 + (1-t)(\bar{\theta}+s)]/2$ and $\Pi = q^*(t)^2$, respectively. Inspection of q^* and Π shows that an unconstrained monopolist prefers complete privacy ($t = 1$) if $s + \bar{\theta} < 0$ and non-privacy ($t = 0$) if the opposite is true. However, the non-negative price constraint will bind if $t < 1$ and s is sufficiently large, and this may induce a monopolist that prefers non-privacy to offer some privacy to relax the constraint.

The quantity associated with a binding constraint ($P = 0$) is $\bar{q}(t) = 1 + (1-t)\bar{\theta}$. The constraint binds if and only if an unconstrained monopolist prefers non-privacy ($s + \bar{\theta} > 0$) and $q^*(0) > \bar{q}(0)$, which is true if $s > 1 + \bar{\theta}$. The constrained monopoly profit is $\bar{\Pi} = (1-t)s[1 + (1-t)\bar{\theta}]$. Differentiating $\bar{\Pi}$ twice yields

$$\bar{\Pi}_t(t) = -s(1 + (1-t)\bar{\theta}), \quad \bar{\Pi}_{tt}(t) = s\bar{\theta}.$$

If $\bar{\theta} < 0$, then $\bar{\Pi}$ is strictly concave in t. For this case, the monopolist's choice of t may have an interior solution. Let $\bar{t}$ be the constrained monopolist's optimal privacy choice. Solving $\bar{\Pi}_t = 0$ yields $\bar{t} = 1 + 1/2\bar{\theta}$ at an interior solution, if one exists. This solution is valid if the non-negative price constraint binds and $\bar{t} \geq 0$, which requires $\bar{\theta} \leq -1/2$. If $\bar{\theta} > -1/2$ and the non-negative price constraint binds, then $\bar{t} = 0$.

Putting these conditions together, the monopolist's optimal privacy choice when faced

---

[31] An example in Farrell (2012) is a special case of the example here.

with a non-negative price constraint is

$$\bar{t} = \begin{cases} 1 & \text{if } \bar{\theta} < -s, \\ 1 + (1/2)\bar{\theta} & \text{if } -s < \bar{\theta} < -1/2, \\ 0 & \text{if } -s < \bar{\theta} \text{ and } -1/2 < \bar{\theta}. \end{cases}$$

When the constraint binds, consumer surplus is $\overline{CS} = (1/2)\bar{q}^2$, and its derivative is $\overline{CS}_t = \bar{q}\bar{q}_t = -\bar{q}\bar{\theta}$. If $-s < \bar{\theta} < -1/2$, then $\bar{\Pi}_t = 0$ (an interior solution) and $\overline{TS}_t = \overline{CS}_t = -\bar{q}\bar{\theta} > 0$, which implies that the monopolist under-supplies privacy. If $-s < \bar{\theta}$ and $-1/2 < \bar{\theta}$, then $\bar{t} = 0$, $\bar{\Pi}_t = -s\bar{q} < 0$, and $\overline{TS}_t = -(s+\bar{\theta})\bar{q} < 0$, which implies that the monopolist makes the efficient choice to offer non-privacy. In all other cases, it is straightforward to show that the monopolist makes the efficient choice.

Figure 1 illustrates how the alignment between private and social preferences for privacy varies with $\bar{\theta}$ and s. Suppose $\bar{\theta} \in [-1,1]$ and $s \in [0,1]$, the region outlined by the rectangular box. This limits the example to cases in which the value of the information and the absolute value of the privacy valuation are no larger than the highest product valuation of any consumer. For all values of s below the line $s = 1 + \bar{\theta}$, the constraint is slack, and private and social preferences are aligned, as expected with linear demand. For values of $(\bar{\theta}, s)$ above the line $s = 1 + \bar{\theta}$, the constraint binds if an unconstrained firm would choose non-privacy, which occurs when $s > -\bar{\theta}$. The shaded region shows the values of $(\bar{\theta}, s)$ such that the profit-maximizing level of privacy is an interior solution and the monopolist under-supplies privacy.

The scope for under-provision in this example is non-trivial. For example, given a flat prior over $\bar{\theta} \in [-1,1]$ and $s \in [0,1]$, a monopolist under-supplies privacy in one-quarter of the cases in which it faces a binding non-negative pricing constraint. In the Appendix, we show that the welfare loss ranges from zero to 8 percent and averages about 5 percent over the shaded region Figure 1.

B. Common Reservation Price

Suppose consumers have a common reservation price $\bar{v}$, and that θ has an arbitrary distribution with cumulative distribution function $F(\theta)$. This is another simple Hotelling-style

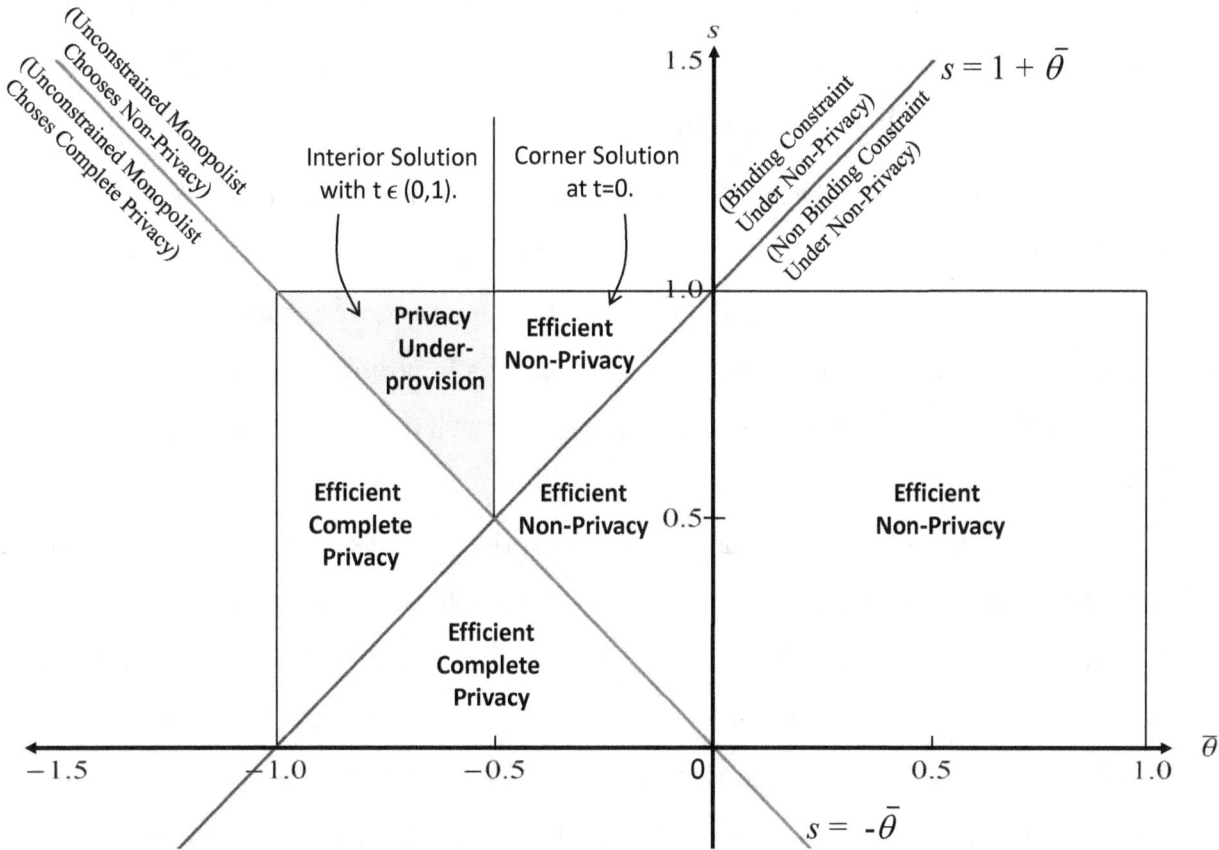

Figure 1: Under-provision of Privacy by a Monopolist Facing a Non-negative Price Constraint

model where customer heterogeneity comes entirely from preferences for privacy. The distribution of $u = \bar{v} + (1-t)\theta$ is $F([\theta - \bar{v}]/(1-t))$, a location-scale family with $\alpha(t) = \bar{v}$ and $\beta(t) = 1 - t$. Inverse demand is $P(q,t) = \bar{v} + (1-t)r(q)$ where $r(q) = F^{-1}(1-q)$. If we think of the information value as part of the demand intercept rather than marginal cost, then the inverse demand is $\tilde{P}(q,t) = \bar{v} + (1-t)s + (1-t)r(q)$.

In this example, the inverse demand $\tilde{P}$ is *variance ordered* in $1-t$ in the terminology of Johnson and Myatt (2006). That is, the scale ("variance") parameter $\beta(t) = 1 - t$ is increasing in $1-t$, which means that raising $1-t$ (reducing t) rotates the inverse demand curve clockwise about some quantity. In addition, $\tilde{P}$ is quasiconvex in $1-t$. Johnson and Myatt show that these conditions imply that the monopoly profit is quasiconvex in $1-t$, which means the monopolist's profit-maximizing choice is an extreme, either $t = 0$ or $t = 1$.

At $t = 1$ the distribution of product valuations becomes degenerate at $\bar{v}$. The monopoly quantity is $q^* = 1$, and the monopoly price is v, which means consumer surplus is zero.

As CS is positive at interior solutions for q, it must be true that $CS_t < 0$ for all q in a neighborhood just below $q = 1$. Therefore, the monopolist does not locally under-supply privacy in this case. It may over-supply privacy, however.

Complete Market Coverage.—The common reservation price case is useful for illustrating the effects of complete market coverage. Although complete coverage may be rare,[32] economists frequently use Hotelling models with complete coverage to analyze a variety of economic questions. Understanding this case may be important for the choice of modeling strategy when conducting any economic analysis in which privacy or other demand attributes are an issue.

When customers have a common reservation price, complete market coverage occurs for sufficiently large t. If F has unbounded support, complete coverage occurs only when $t = 1$. If F has bounded support, then there is some t' such that marginal revenue intersects the vertical line at $q = 1$ at prices above marginal cost for all $t \geq t'$. For all such t, $q^* = 1$. Propositions 2 through 5 are informative if the monopolist's optimal privacy choice is $t = 0$, but not if its optimal choice is $t = 1$. In the latter case, we have shown that the monopolist may over-supply privacy, but does not under-supply it. We conclude that models with complete market coverage are biased toward predicting the over-supply of privacy.

C. Uniformly Distributed and Correlated Valuations for the Product and Privacy

Demand is linear if either v or θ has a uniform distribution and the other is a scaler, as in cases A and B. A richer example of linear demand occurs when v is uniformly distributed between zero and 1 and $\theta = \gamma v$, where $\gamma \in [-1, 1]$. This is a simple way to capture correlation between v and θ, with a positive (negative) correlation arising when γ is greater than (less than) zero. In this case, $u = v(1+\gamma(1-t))$, which is uniformly distributed on $[0, 1+\gamma(1-t)]$. This is a location-scale family with $\alpha(t) = \gamma(1-t)$, $\beta(t) = 1$, and $r(q) = 1-q$. Because privacy shifts only the location parameter, it follows from Proposition 2 that private and social preferences are aligned at an interior solution.

---

[32] Consider, however, that virtually every consumer with an internet connection engages in online activity that conveys information to the internet provider.

This example illustrates that a positive or negative correlation between v and θ is *not* sufficient to generate a misalignment between private and social preferences. At interior solutions, correlation yields distortions only if it generates demand curvature and changes in policy affect scale. A binding non-negative price constraint would also give rise to distortions in this example, as in case A.

D. Normally Distributed Valuations for the Product and Privacy

Cases A-C illustrate Propositions 2, 3, and 5. We now provide an example based on normally distributed preferences for the product and privacy that illustrates Proposition 4.

It is worth stating the primary reasons why the normal case is attractive. If v and θ each arise from aggregating the values of a large number of attributes drawn from a common joint distribution, then they will be approximately multivariate normally distributed by the central limit theorem. Absent specific knowledge about the distributions of v, θ, and u, normality would seem to be the most reasonable assumption. In addition, two convenient properties of the normal distribution are that location and scale parameters are the mean and standard deviation of the distribution, and the weighted sum of two normal random variables is also normal. This makes the normal case convenient for applications, as conclusions depend on a few parameters that have simple interpretations. Let $(\bar{v}, \bar{\theta})$ and $(\sigma_v^2, \sigma_\theta^2)$ be the means and variances of v and θ, and let ρ be the correlation coefficient. Then $u = v + (1-t)\theta$ is normally distributed with mean $\mu(t) = \bar{v} + (1-t)\bar{\theta}$ and variance $\sigma^2(t) = \sigma_v^2 + (1-t)^2\sigma_\theta^2 + 2(1-t)\sigma_v\sigma_\theta\rho$.

As noted earlier, when u is normally distributed, the global incidence exceeds the local incidence for all values of marginal cost. Therefore, by Proposition 4, a monopolist that is not constrained by a zero lower price bound does not under-supply privacy that reduces the variance, and it does not over-supply privacy that increases the variance. Differentiating σ^2 shows that the variances falls (rises) with t as $-\rho > (<) (1-t)\sigma_\theta/\sigma_v$. This yields the following proposition.

Proposition 6 *Suppose valuations for the product and privacy are multivariate normally distributed. If the monopolist does not face a binding non-negative price constraint, then the* *following statement is true:*

$$-\rho \begin{matrix} > \\ < \end{matrix} \left[\frac{(1-t)\sigma_\theta}{\sigma_v}\right] \implies \begin{matrix} \text{No Under-supply} \\ \text{No Over-supply} \end{matrix}$$

Proposition 6 implies that a necessary condition for the under-supply of privacy at interior solutions is a sufficiently large positive correlation between consumers' valuations for the product and privacy.[33]

The sign of the inequality in Proposition 6 is obviously an empirical question. In many cases there may be no reason to believe without evidence that the correlation is either positive or negative. However, one can also imagine scenarios where consumers' product and privacy valuations are positively correlated, possibly strongly so. One example may be the privacy of health care information. Consumers that are sick likely place high value on health care, and they may also have strong desires to keep information about their health confidential to avoid possible discrimination by employers or other third parties.[34] Other examples might be online activities considered by some to constitute questionable behavior (e.g., gambling, pornography, certain types of social interaction). Consumers who place high value on such activities may also place high value on keeping their information private to prevent third parties from forming opinions about them that they might not like. Proposition 6 indicates that if the correlation between product and privacy valuations in these cases is high enough, then the firm will under-supply privacy.

The Size and Scope of Distortions in the Multivariate Normal Case.—Whichever inequality in Proposition 6 is true, Propositions 4 and 5 imply that there may be a distortion in the opposite direction. We are interested in how frequently distortions occur and how big they can be in the multivariate normal case, with and without a non-negative price constraint.

Addressing these questions requires numerical methods, as the normal distribution does not have a closed form. Our objective was to consider a range of parameters that represent plausible markets for purchases that have privacy implications. To achieve this, we took

---

[33] Recall that $-\theta$ is customer θ's privacy valuation, so $-\rho$ is the correlation between customers' valuations for the product and privacy.

[34] This point pertains to health care purchases from physical locations (hospitals, doctors offices, drugstores) as well as online.

two million draws from a uniform distribution with the parameters covering the following ranges: $s \in [0, 10]$, $v \in [0, 10]$, $\sigma_v \in [.05, 10]$, $\bar{\theta} \in [-10, 10]$, $\sigma_\theta^2 \in [.05, 10]$, and $\rho \in [-.99, .99]$. We normalized c to zero. The result is a distribution of markets with a wide range of characteristics, which we now describe.

The average value of privacy $(-\bar{\theta})$ may be many times higher or many times lower in absolute value than the value of the product. For example, the product may have an average value near ten but a privacy value near zero, or the opposite may be true. An example of a case when the average product value may be high relative to the average privacy value might be web browsing that leads to a few unwanted advertisements in the absence of privacy. An example of a case when the average product value is low relative to the average privacy value might be an online purchase that could have easily been made off line leads to a flood of advertisements from several firms that partner with the seller.

The value of the information covers the same range as the average value of the product, allowing it to be potentially very high or very low relative to either or both the average values of the product and privacy. An example of high information value relative to product value might be certain web browsing, which is generally offered for free because of the value firms derive from the opportunity to present advertisements to the customer. An example where the information value may be low relative to the product value might be the purchase of an expensive product over the internet.

The variance of the product and privacy valuations affect the elasticity of the aggregate demand curve. By allowing both variances to range from low to high, the model permits most relevant combinations of demand elasticities across regimes. The correlation between the value of the product and the privacy externality covers the range of possibilities between -1 and 1. Our objective is simply to consider the full range of possibilities.[35]

Table 1 summarizes the welfare results from our simulations, where we treated the privacy decision a discrete choice of $t = 0$ or $t = 1$. We report averages across all markets and constrained markets, where the monopolist faces a binding non-negative price constraint under non-privacy.

---

[35]The distribution of parameters we are considering is inherently somewhat arbitrary. We cannot claim that the distribution induced over outcomes is representative of the distribution of outcomes in real markets. Our objective is simply to consider a range of cases that include plausible cases we can imagine.

Table 1: Summary of Normal Simulation Welfare Results

Condition	All Markets (N=2 million) (%)	Constrained Markets (N=36,992) (%)
Privacy increases welfare	16.53	73.39
Privacy under-supplied	0.45	3.72
Privacy over-supplied	0.93	1.31
Mean welfare cost of imposing unconditional privacy	50.64	11.67
Mean welfare benefit of correcting under-supply	3.35	11.20

Notes: Welfare costs and benefits are percentage changes.

Across all 2 million cases, both the frequency and welfare cost from under-supply appear rather insignificant. The firm fails to supply privacy when the planner wants it in only one half of one percent of the cases. The benefit from identifying and correcting under-supply averages just over 3 percent across all cases in which under-supply occurs. Globally imposing privacy in lieu of the firm's choice reduces welfare by a large amount—about 51 percent on average. The relative infrequency and small magnitude of the distortions in this simulation occurs because demand derived from the normal distribution is reasonably close to linear over much of its range, and the constraint binds in our simulation less than 2 percent ($\approx 36,992/2,000,000$) of the time.[36]

A binding price constraint significantly increases the frequency of under-supply and the potential benefits from correcting it, and it reduces the average welfare cost of imposing privacy globally in lieu of the firm's decision. In our simulation, the firm under-supplies privacy in just under 4 percent of the constrained cases, compared to one-half of one percent across all cases. Imposing privacy unconditionally has a much smaller average welfare cost—about 12 percent in constrained markets compared with 51 percent across all markets—and the average benefit of identifying and correcting under-supply is greater—about 11 percent in constrained markets compared to 3 percent in all markets.

---

[36]These conclusions do not change significantly if we confine attention to cases where the average privacy externality $\bar{\theta}$ is non-positive. The reason is that the monopolist's preferences for privacy correlate well with those of consumers because demand is reasonably close to linear.

Of course, this simulation is an example based on flat priors across the specific parameter grid we assumed. The main conclusions we draw from this example are: (1) in the abstract, it seems likely that a monopolist will frequently make socially desirable privacy decisions, and (2) a binding non-negative price constraint increases the benefits of identifying and correcting under-supply and reduces the costs of wrongly imposing privacy where it is harmful.

V. Other Applications

We now discuss the implications of our results for the welfare analysis other non-price decisions that generate demand rotations. The applications include product design, disclosure, and advertising. We also discuss the implications of our results for the use of linear models in applied work.

In each application an increase in the product attribute can be interpreted as a reduction in privacy in the context of our model. Let $a = 1 - t$ be the amount of the attribute, so that $u = v + a\theta$, and let $\alpha(a)$ and $\beta(a)$ be the demand parameters. Let the marginal cost component associated with the attribute be as (rather than $-(1-t)s$),[37] and define the over- and under-supply of a as in Definition 1, replacing t with a. It is straightforward to show that the analog of condition (17) for assessing whether a monopolist over-supplies or under-supplies the attribute is then the same as (17) with the derivatives being with respect to a instead of t:

$$(18) \qquad TS_a = \frac{\beta_a}{\beta}[\Pi + K]\left[\tau^{GV} - \tau\right] + (1+\tau)\Pi_a + \tau K_a.$$

Here, $K = K_a = 0$ if changes in a do not affect fixed costs. Otherwise both are positive.

A. Product Design

Johnson and Myatt (2006) show that product design can be viewed as choosing the dispersion of the customer preference distribution by choosing the amounts of different product characteristics to include in the design. In our model, we can think of $a\theta$ as the utility associated with the amount a of a single additional characteristic. All of our welfare results

---
[37]None of our results change with the sign of this component of marginal cost.

are applicable to the question of whether a monopolist over-supplies or under-supplies a particular characteristic θ in the design. As with privacy, a misalignment between monopoly and social incentives for a new design requires: (1) the presence of demand curvature that causes a divergence between the local and global incidences (assuming no price constraints and incomplete market coverage); and (2) design changes cause changes in scale (dispersion).

B. Information Disclosure

One way that firms attempt to make their products more valuable to customers is by disclosing information that has the potential to improve the user experience. For example, suppliers of mobile devices, personal computers, software, etc., must decide what information to disclose about how to use their products, and how to disclose it. In many cases, these decisions involve tradeoffs. For example, on-screen explanations of how to use a product may be helpful to some users, but may harm others by bogging down their experience. In this context, information disclosure rotates demand, benefitting some consumers and harming others. A policy question is how well firms' incentives to disclose information align with social incentives.[38]

The disclosure of information that affects the user-experience is the flip side of privacy in our model. The choice of privacy level t is analogous to a product design decision to provide the amount of disclosure $a = (1-t)$, which is essentially a characteristic in the design.[39] Our welfare results are applicable to this issue in the same way they are applicable to product design.

C. Advertising

Bagwell's (2007) survey of the advertising literature classifies advertising into three types for the purposes of normative analysis: persuasive, informative, and complementary. Informative advertising conveys valuable information to consumers, while complementary advertising

---

[38] This tradeoff between the benefits and costs of additional disclosure was a central issue in the Federal Trade Commission's settlement with Apple for its disclosure practices relating to In-App purchases for games played on the iPhone and iPad. See In the Matter of Apple, Inc., FTC File No. 1123108, January 15, 2014, http://www.ftc.gov/enforcement/cases-proceedings/112-3108/apple-inc.

[39] As with privacy, application of our model to disclosure assumes that the nature and effects of disclosure are common knowledge.

enters consumers' utility functions in a way that is complementary to the consumption of the advertised product. In both cases advertising shifts or rotates demand, and consumer surplus provides a valid measure of consumer welfare absent income effects (as we assume in our model).[40]

To apply our model to the advertising question, interpret $a = 1 - t$ as the amount of advertising. An increase in advertising is then analogous to a reduction in privacy that benefits consumers with $\theta > 0$ and hurts consumers with $\theta < 0$. Propositions 2 through 5 are applicable.

Advertising is one activity that is likely to affect fixed costs in addition to or instead of marginal costs. Our analysis in Section III.F, which incorporates fixed costs, provides necessary and sufficient conditions for the under-provision of advertising that have not appeared in the literature. Specifically, condition (18) implies the following proposition.

Proposition 7 *Suppose advertising strictly increases fixed costs, $K_a > 0$, and that the monopoly advertising decision has an interior solution ($\Pi_a = 0$). Then if β_a and $[\tau^{GV} - \tau]$ have the same sign (weakly), the monopolist under-supplies advertising. If demand is linear ($\tau^{GV} - \tau = 0$), then the monopolist under-supplies advertising.*

Bagwell (2007) showed that a sufficient condition for too little advertising is that $P_{aq} < 0$ and $q_a^* \geq 0$. Proposition 7 provides a weaker sufficient condition for the under-supply of advertising when demand is from the location-scale family. In particular, P_{aq} has the same sign as $-\beta_a$, yet under-supply can occur whether β_a is positive or negative. For distributions such that $[\tau^{GV} - \tau] > 0$, as with the normal and logistic, the sufficient condition for under-supply is $\beta_a > 0$, which for the location-scale class is equivalent to Bagwell's condition that $P_{aq} < 0$. If the global incidence is less than the local incidence, then advertising that reduces scale, $\beta_a < 0$, is also under-supplied.

D. Implications for the Use of Linear Models in Applied Work

Proposition 3 has startling implications for the frequent practice in applied work of linearizing functions to make analysis easier. For example, a common practice in merger analysis is to

---

[40]Persuasive advertising is less conducive to welfare analysis, as consumers may make purchases that are not utility maximizing.

use first order approximations to predict merger-induced price changes. The underlying assumption is that linear approximations are reasonable.

The validity of assuming linearity is context specific. Proposition 3 implies that this assumption is far from innocuous when analyzing the welfare effects of firms' private decisions over the supply of product attributes. If one assumes linear demand for this question, and if the pricing problem has an interior solution, then the welfare question becomes moot. Clearly, an understanding of the nature and effects of demand curvature is required for rational policy toward firms' private decisions about product attributes.[41] This requirement may not be as dire as it sounds, as the use of a specific preference distribution (or representative utility function) in a particular empirical analysis typically imposes enough structure to draw conclusions based on a few parameters that can be empirically estimated. Of course, an empirical analysis that imposes curvature that does not exist is likely to yield invalid estimates and conclusions. An open question is when the data are good enough to identify demand curvature well enough for use in policy toward demand attributes.

VI. Conclusion

We have explored the private and social incentives for privacy in a model in which product purchases convey information about customers, the information is valuable to sellers, and the sale or use of customer information generates externalities that may affect different customers in different ways. The use of customer-specific information is not mediated directly by the price system, leaving open the possibility that externalities from non-privacy might lead to socially suboptimal outcomes. The main question we addressed is whether firms have the right incentives to offer privacy in this environment.

Given the inability to write contracts on a customer-by-customer basis, privacy becomes a product attribute that rotates aggregate demand, potentially benefitting some customers and harming others. Our analysis provides a new welfare analysis of demand rotations that yields insights not only for questions about privacy, but also for other demand attribute

---

[41]The assumption of linearity is less problematic in the merger context, as predictions from linear models tend to vary with parameters in ways predicted by the theory. However, that literature also recognizes the benefits of predictions that either do not depend on demand curvature (Werden, 1996) or that take curvature into account (Jaffe and Weyl, 2013).

decisions that rotate demand.

As regards privacy, we explicitly assume that firms keep their privacy commitments, and that these commitments are understood by consumers. The assumption that privacy policies are common knowledge is important in our model, as firms have short run incentives to renege on their commitments. If reputation effects are deemed too weak to support long run commitments, then an obvious potential role for a regulator is to ensure that the privacy commitments firms make are kept.

In our setting, we find that firms in competitive markets offer customers the option of privacy whenever it is socially optimal to do so, while a monopolist may or may not make the socially optimal choice. One lesson is that effective competition policy is one tool for encouraging firms to make socially beneficial privacy choices.

Under monopoly, we provide necessary and sufficient conditions for the monopolist to under-supply or over-supply privacy. For the case of normally distributed valuations, we present a simulation based on flat priors over a plausible parameter space. In this example, a monopolist makes the socially optimal choice between privacy and non-privacy in over 99 percent of the cases, and the welfare cost of imposing privacy unconditionally is quite large. This finding, combined with the empirical results of Goldfarb and Tucker (2011), suggest that regulatory authorities should be cautious when considering the imposition of specific privacy provisions. Our results also imply that the scope for under-provision is higher when the firm faces a binding non-negative price constraint. This suggests that markets with zero marginal price (e.g., web browsing) may be more likely to benefit from privacy regulation, although the frequency of under-provision in our simulation for the case of normally distributed valuations is under 5 percent even when limited to cases in which the non-negative price constraint binds.

An issue we do not address in this paper is the incentive for a monopolist to offer consumers the option of different levels of privacy protection, possibly at different prices. For example, firms frequently allow consumers to opt out of receiving advertisements through email. We also see examples of firms charging higher prices for services that come without advertisements than they charge for the same services accompanied by advertisements. An important potential extension would compare the private and social incentives for optional privacy policies in environments in which privacy rotates demand.

The success of privacy commitments relies on disclosures by firms that are clear and easy to understand. In the abstraction embodied by our model, the meaning of privacy is clear: privacy means that the firm will use or sell certain customer information that imposes externalities (positive or negative) on consumers. In the real world, privacy commitments are more complex, and customers incur a cost in trying to understand exactly what they mean. It is not obvious whether firms have private incentives to develop principles or standards that ensure optimal transparency. Even if they have such incentives, the coordination required to make this happen may be costly and may entail other risks (e.g., anticompetitive collusion). The feasibility of transparent privacy policies and the incentives for firms to provide them are important topics topics for further research.

REFERENCES

Acquisti, Alessandro, and Hal R. Varian (2005), "Conditioning Prices on Purchase History," *Marketing Science* 24:3, 367-381.

Anderson, Simon, de Palma, Andre, and Brent Kreider (2001), "The Efficiency of Indirect Taxes under Imperfect Compeitition," *Journal of Public Economics*, 81, 231-251.

Bagwell, Kyle, "The Economic Analysis of Advertising," in *Handbook of Industrial Organization*, Armstrong, Mark and Robert Porter, eds., Volume 3, 2007, Elsevier, 1701-1844.

Becker, Gary S. and Kevin M. Murphy (1993), "A Simple Theory of Advertising as a Good or Bad," *Quarterly Journal of Economics*, 108:4, 941-964.

Bulow, Jeremy I., and Paul Pfleiderer (1983), "A Note on the Effect of Cost Changes on Prices," *The Journal of Political Economy*, 91.1, 182-185.

Calzolari, Giacomo, and Alessandro Pavan (2006), "On the optimality of privacy in sequential contracting," *Journal of Economic Theory*, 130:1, 168-204.

Coase, Ronald (1960), "The Problem of Social Cost," *Journal of Law and Economics*, 3(1), 1-44.

Dixit, Avinansh and Norman, Victor (1978), "Advertising and Welfare," *Bell Journal of Economics*, 9(9), 1-17.

Fabinger, Michal, and Weyl, Glen (2012), "Pass-Through and Demand Forms," Working Paper, University of Chicago.

Fabinger, Michal, and Weyl, Glen (2013), "Pass-Through as an Economic Tool: Principles of Incidence under Imperfect Comptition," *Journal of Political Economy*, 121(3), 528-583.

Farrell, Joseph (2012), "Can Privacy be Just Another Good?" *Journal on Telecommunications & High Technology Law*, 10, 251.

Goldfarb, Avi, and Catherine E. Tucker (2011), "Privacy Regulation and Online Advertising," *Management Science*, 57(1), 57-71.

Hermalin, Benjamin E. and Michael L. Katz (2006), "Privacy, Property Rights and Efficiency: The Economics of Privacy as Secrecy," *Quantitative Marketing and Economics*, 4:3, 209-239.

Jaffe, Sonia, and E. Glen Weyl (2013), "The First Order Approach to Merger Analysis," *American Economic Journal: Microeconomics*, 5(4), 188-218.

Johnson, Justin P. and David P. Myatt (2006), "On the Simple Economics of Advertising, Marketing, and Product Design," *American Economic Review*, 96(3), 756-784.

Kotowitz, Yehuda and Frank (1979), "Advertising, Consumer Information, and Product Quality," *Bell Journal of Economics*, 2, 566-588.

Laudon, Kenneth C. (1996) "Markets and Privacy," *Communications of the ACM*, 39(9), September 1996, 92-104.

Lenard, Thomas M. and Paul H. Rubin (2009), "In Defense of Data: Information and the Cost of Privacy," Technology Policy Institute Working Paper, Emory Law and Economics Research Paper No. 9-44, May 18, 2009, available at SSRN: http://ssrn.com/ abstract=1407731 or http://dx.doi.org/10.2139/ssrn.1407731.

Letter from U.S. NGOs to U.S. Government Leaders ("On the Need to Modernize and Update EU and US Privacy Law"), February 4, 2013, available at http://www.centerfordigitaldemocracy.org/digital-privacy.

Schmalensee, Richard, "Gaussian Demand and Commodity Bundling," *The Journal of Business*, 57(1) Part 2, S211-S230.

Shapiro, Carl (1980), "Advertising and Welfare: Comment," *Bell Journal of Economics*, 12(2), 749-751.

Sheshinski, Eytan (1976), "Price, Quality and Quantity Regulation in Monopoly Situations," *Economica* 43:170, 127-137.

Spence, A. Michael (1975), "Monopoly, Quality, and Regulation," *The Bell Journal of Economics*, 6:2, Autumn, 417-429.

Taylor, Curtis R. (2004) "Consumer Privacy and the Market for Customer Information." *Rand Journal of Economics*, 35:4, Winter, 631-650.

Tucker, Catherine (2010), "The Economics Value of Online Customer Data," Background Paper #1, OECD Roundtable: *The Economics of Personal Data Privacy: 30 Years after the OECD Privacy Guidelines*, December 1, 2010, available at http://www.oecd.org/sti/ieconomy/46968839.pdf.

Werden, Gregory J. (1996), "A Robust Test for Consumer Welfare Enhancing Mergers Among Sellers of Differentiated Products," *The Journal of Industrial Economics*, 44(4), 409-413.

Varian, Hal R. (1996), "Economic Aspects of Personal Privacy," mimeo, U.C. Berkeley, December 6, 1996.

Appendix

Propositions 1-3, 6 and 7 are proved in the text. This appendix provides a formal proof of Propositions 4 and 5. It also presents calculations of the welfare losses associated with the under-provision of privacy in the example in Section IV.B.

Proof of Proposition 4.

Part 1. Note that $\hat{\Pi} \geq 0$ and $\tau \geq 0$. Suppose $\beta_t < 0$. The under-supply of privacy requires $\Pi_t < 0$. By condition (10), if $CS/\Pi \geq \tau$, then $CS_t \leq 0$, which is inconsistent with under-supply. This establishes 1a. Parts 1b-1d follow from analogous arguments.

Part 2. The result will hold if it is possible to choose α_t so that $\Pi_t = 0$ without violating the premises in 1a-1d. If this is possible, condition (12) implies either over-supply or under-supply, depending on the signs of β_t and $\tau^G - \tau$.

Using (8), $\Pi_t = 0$ if $\hat{c}_t = \beta_t \hat{\Pi}/\beta q^*$. Differentiating $\hat{c} = [c - (1-t)s - \alpha(t)]/\beta(t)$ yields $\hat{c}_t = (s - \alpha_t)/\beta - \beta_t \hat{c}/\beta$. Changes in α_t do not affect values of β, $\hat{\Pi}$, $\hat{CS}$, q^*, and τ, which pin down the premises in 1a-1d. Therefore, it is possible to choose α_t to adjust $\hat{c}_t$ so that $\Pi_t = 0$ without violating the premises in 1a-1d. Q.E.D.

Proof of Proposition (5).

Part 1. Given $\beta_t = 0$, $\eta_t = \beta \lambda_t$, and the adjusted incidence difference in square brackets is $-\tau/(1+\lambda) < 0$. Therefore, the first term in (16) the has the opposite sign of λ_t. If $\lambda_t < 0$, the first term is positive, and there is no distortion if $\overline{\Pi} > 0$, which implies no over-supply (part b). If $\overline{\Pi} < 0$, the first term is negative, and there is no distortion if $\overline{\Pi} > 0$, which implies no over-supply.

Part 2. The example in Section IV.A with the binding non-negative price constraint proves part 2 of the proposition. In that example, $\alpha_t = -\bar{\theta}$, and the example shows that there exist values of $(\bar{\theta}, s)$ such that the firm under-supplies privacy. Q.E.D.

Welfare Cost of Under-supply in the Example in Section IV.A

Over the shaded region in Figure 1, the monopolist's profit-maximizing privacy level is an interior solution at $\bar{t} = 1 + 1/(2\bar{\theta})$. The planner would like to raise t. We first show that total surplus is maximized by raising t until the non-negative price constraint is just relaxed. We then express the welfare loss.

Under a binding non-negative pricing constraint, quantity is $\bar{q} = 1 + (1-t)\bar{\theta}$, profit is $\bar{\Pi} = s(1-t)\bar{q}$ and consumer surplus is $(1/2)\bar{q}^2$. Total surplus is therefore

$$\overline{TS} = s(1-t)\bar{q} + (1/2)\bar{q}^2.$$

Differentiating $\overline{TS}$ twice yields

$$\overline{TS}_t = -(s+\bar{\theta})\bar{q} + (1-t)s\bar{\theta}, \quad \overline{TS}_{tt} = \bar{\theta}(2s+\bar{\theta}).$$

In the relevant range where $-s < \bar{\theta} < -1/2$, $\overline{TS}_{tt} < 0$, which means $\overline{TS}$ is concave and could have an interior maximum. Solving $\overline{TS}_t = 0$ for t yields

$$t^{TSMax} = 1 + \frac{s+\bar{\theta}}{\bar{\theta}(2s+\bar{\theta})}$$

Evaluating $\bar{q}$ and q^* at t^{TSMax} shows that

$$\bar{q}(t^{TSMax}) - q^*(t^{TSMax}) = \left(\frac{s}{2\bar{\theta}}\right)\left(\frac{s+2\bar{\theta}}{2s+\bar{\theta}}\right) > 0.$$

This means that the total surplus maximizing level of t must fully relax the constraint. Note that t^{TSMax} goes too far, however, as the planner does not want to do more than relax the constraint in the region where $s+\bar{\theta} > 0$. This is true because both the planner and the firm would prefer non-privacy in this region if there were no constraint.

The value of t at which the the constraint just relaxes is found by solving $\bar{q}(t) = q^*(t)$, which gives

$$t^{Relaxed} = 1 + \frac{1}{\bar{\theta} - s},$$

which lies between zero and one for values of s and $\bar{\theta}$ in the relevant range. The welfare loss from under-provision is the difference between total surplus at $t = t^{Relax}$ and total surplus at $t = \bar{t}$. Algebra that would be exceptionally tedious but for Mathematic shows that the percentage welfare loss in the relevant region is

$$\frac{\overline{TS}(t^{Relaxed}) - \overline{TS}(\bar{t})}{\overline{TS}(\bar{t})} = -\frac{(s+\bar{\theta})(2s^2 + 5s\bar{\theta} - \bar{\theta}^2)}{(s-\bar{\theta})^2(2s-\bar{\theta})}$$

The welfare losses is plotted in Figure 2. Integrating over the region $-1 < -s < \bar{\theta} < -1/2$ using Mathematica and dividing by $1/8$ yields an average welfare loss of 4.97 percent over the region in which the non-negative price constraint binds.

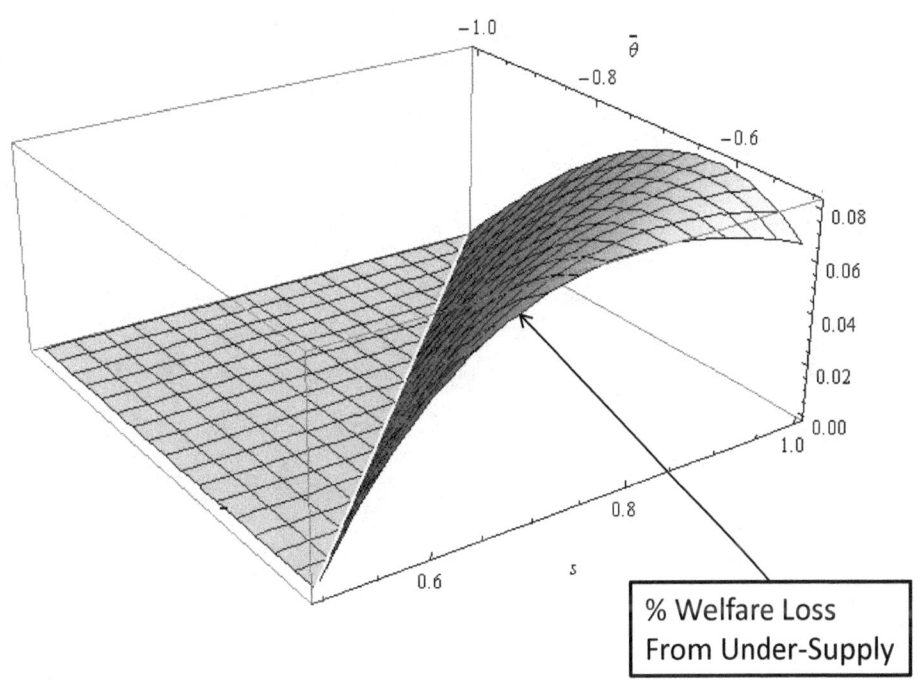

Figure 2: Welfare Loss from Under-provision of Privacy in Linear Example of Monopolist Facing Binding Non-negative Price Constraint

www.ingramcontent.com/pod-product-compliance
Lightning Source LLC
Chambersburg PA
CBHW081800170526
45167CB00008B/3268